A SELF - HELP BOOK FOR TODAY'S BUSY WORLD

Life is Simple

✚

Compiled & Written
by
Henry Hamer

"life is really SIMPLE but we insist on making it complicated."

*"THIS BOOKLET WILL HELP; YOU ADD MORE
ZEST TO YOUR LIFE."
MAKE IT LESS COMPLICATED.."*

INDEX

85. Anxiety
94. Appreciation
84 Attitude
59. Brain
101. Caring
111 Choices
101. Compassion
6. Comments
7. Concentrate
92. Confidence
79. Critical think-
99. Declaration of
111 Decisions
68. Education
75. Emotions
101. Empathy
13. **Ethics***
81 Evil

93. Failure
85. Fear
54. Freedom
7. Focus
19. **Goals***

23. **<u>Happiness</u>****
26. (What is)
28. (Why)
29. (Pursuit)
30. (No Limits).
31. Choose
32. (Achieve)
34 (Impedes)
39 (People)
41. (Appreciate)
43. (Pleasure)
47. (Never)

48 Habits
117. Health
71. How to think
67. Intelligence
4. Introduction
67. Knowledge
10. Life is easy
8. Life is Simple
115. Luck
104 Mentors
13. **Morality***
109. Motivation
11. **Philosophy***
22 Oprimiam
58 Placebo
80 Positive
74. Procrastinate

53. Purpose
51. **Reason**
82. Rationalizing
97. Relationships
49. Self Esteem
49. Self Worth
89. Stress
105 Success
83. Suffering
80 Thinking
52 Time
56. Truth
95. Value
88 Worry
69. Wisdom

*   7.   How to use this Book
* 18.   Common Morality
*
*

This book is

Dedicated to you

Helping you find more Happiness

in your Life.

PUBLISHER'S NOTE

The ideas, procedures, and suggestions
contained in this book are not intended as
a substitute for consulting with your physician.

ALL MATTERS REGARDING YOUR HEALTH REQUIRE
MEDICAL SUPERVISION.

October 15 2022

INTRODUCTION

Life is Simple booklet does not promise Miracles,
Secrets, or ask you to tap into some Hidden Power.

Life is Simple booklet is a compilation of some thoughts,
reminders, and ideas which, if put into practice,
will make your life easier, increase your happiness
and enhance your unique individuality.

Life is Simple booklet is written for the majority of people
whose lives are far too busy to read lengthy Self-Help Books.
Please note: <u>There are no inspirational stories in this book.</u>

I hope this common sense booklet
will be helpful to you and also give you a understanding of
others so you can deal with them effectively.
I recommend Dennis Prager University - *Henry.*

"Life itself is simple….it's just not easy."
Steve Maraboli

"Many people are so desperately unhappy that they will snatch up anything offering hope or simply offering quick-and-easy wealth. My question is, who will be there to pick up the pieces when they discover that they bought into a lie? And who will help the people who believe that they brought every misfortune on themselves because they sent negative thoughts and feeling out into the universe like a human radio transmitter."   Professor Robert Thompson Syracuse University.

PLEASE NOTE THE FOLLOWING

<u>WITHOUT GOOD HEALTH</u>
<u>LIFE IS VERY DIFFICULT</u>

When we are young we take our health for granted.
It is never to late to improve our health.
(First you have to see a Medical Doctor.)

For Good health.you need to do the following:-

1. Thinking young in a mature way, is a must.

2.Taking action when stressed is a must.
(Deep breathing helps stress.)

3.Moderate Exercise is a must.

4. No process foods is a must.
Mediterranean diet seams to be best.

5. Confidence in one's self is very important.
The following pages is a confidence builder.

LAUGHING EVERY DAY
Puts you in a good mood.
(Even if you have to laugh by yourself do it -
laugh out loud.)

COMMENTS

A very powerful booklet. I would like to give all my students a copy.
R.R.H Professor of Psychology. LMU/LA.

I loved your book Henry it was Fabulous.
It's going to be the book that I bring out from time to time and read a chapter or
two to get me back in tune with Life's ups and downs.
Trish. New Zealand.

Henry, Thank you for sharing your book "Life is Simple" with me.
It is a wonderful synthesis of the many facets of life whose Complexity when
intertwined as a whole makes it impossible to separate out the pieces in order to
begins the tall task of making necessary repairs. Readers can approach the
<u>book as a whole or in pieces making it even more digestible.</u>
C.L.A. Los Angeles. Teacher.

Henry I would like to commend you on the writing of your book "Life is Simple."
As an experienced educator, of 33 years. I have been expose to all sorts of books,
Pamphlets, reading, scriptures to name a few. There comes a time in my life when
I would yearn for someone to teach me instead of my teaching them.   You Henry,
fulfilled something I realized was missing. From the time I opened your book on the
flight home, I could not put it down. Every chapter I read put a piece of the pie back
together for me.   Not only did your writing teach me appreciate the
contents of your book, but most of all to live through your works, "Life is Simple."
I want to thank you for giving me the honor to read your creation and believe that
every person at some time in their life should experience reading your book.
I know it would provide people the ability not to complicate what doesn't matter in
life but to live it simple and take time to appreciate what life should be all about.
K.D. Educator of the year New Jersey.

HOW TO USE THIS BOOK

Read this booklet slowly.

FOCUS
CONCENTRATE

Think about what you are reading.

Do not let your mind wander.

Do not start reading this book if
you are going to be distracted.
Turn of the music.

<u>Underline</u> items you want to emphasize and **<u>works for you.</u>**

Read *Life is Simple Booklet* often to increase your happiness.

***

LIFE IS SIMPLE

WHAT IS COMPLICATED IS HOW LIFE WORKS
All you have to do is -

HAVE GOOD HEALTH

HAVE A PHILOSOPHY

HAVE ETHICS & MORALITY

HAVE GOOD VALUES

SET GOALS
This will build the foundation for a better life.

If you work on these five things,
your brain will automatically
use the power of reason to take the
necessary action to achieve a happier and better life.

"Everything is Simple; it's people who make life complicated."
Twitter.

Life is a challenge;
this book will help you deal with life challenges
****

LET THIS BOOKLET
AND
YOUR BRAIN WORK FOR YOU.

Your self-esteem / self-worth will rise.
You will have meaning and purpose in your life.
You will be learning more and will be more
motivated to achieve your goals.

You will be making better choices,
and you will become a happier person.
You will be healthier in body and mind,
and this is just for starters.

~~~

<u>There are events that will affect you,
which you cannot control.</u>
In response you have to use your brain to make these
events benefit your life by dealing with them effectively.
Remember not everything in life goes right or
is perfect, or can be set right.

*"The man of authentic self-confidence is the man who
relies on the judgment of his mind.   Ayn Rand.~*

***How you act is how you feel,
Don't let feelings make you act. Dennis Prager***

Your Brain is the most powerful tool you have use it.
~~~

LIFE IS EASY

(If you find life hard it is of your own making most of the time.)

The Key to life is improving it.

THE KEY
TO HAPPINESS
IS HAVING

<u>*GOOD HEALTH*</u>
<u>*A PHILOSOPHY*</u>
<u>*ETHICS* - *MORALITY*</u>
<u>GOOD VALUES</u>
<u>*PURPOSE* - *GOALS* - *WISDOM*</u>
<u>*DISCIPLINE*</u>

and integrating them together.

You must be able to avoid
disagreements between your
Philosophy,
Ethics - Morality - Purpose - Goals - Wisdom Discipline.

It is never too late to make changes.
***

~ PHILOSOPHY ~

The code of conduct as to how we live is Philosophy.
"Philosophy the Rules for conduct of life…" Oxford dictionary.

We all need something to believe in;
that is why we have to have our own philosophy.

Moral Religions give us Rules for conduct of life.

THIS BOOK
WILL HELP YOU CHOOSE THE RIGHT ASSETS
TO IMPROVE YOUR PHILOSOPHY
LEADING TO A HAPPIER LIFE.

Once you have the rules for your conduct firmly imprinted
into your brain your life will go much more smoothly.

**Imagine playing a game without rules
You would not be able to play.**
Without rules life goes off in too many directions
without any control, preventing you from being happy.

Ask yourself what is the meaning of Life and your Life?
What is your purpose for living?
Your Philosophy should give you the answer.

Your Philosophy must be built on a foundation of
Ethics, Morality, respecting others and doing the moral right thing.
You must consider these things in all your actions.

Believing in individualism
and not subscribing to Collectivism
will enhance your Happiness and bring more peace to Society
and therefore should be part of your Philosophy.

*"Our philosophy, in essence, should be the concept of man
as a heroic being with his own happiness
as the moral purpose of his life, with productive achievements
as his nobles activity and reason as his only absolute."*
                                                    Ayn Rand.

Embracing the Objectivism Philosophy
as your own will save you time and effort
in making up your own Philosophy.

Objectivism is a modern and up-to-date Philosophy.
Why embrace a primitive Philosophy that may
or may not apply in today's world?

Read the 'Ayn Rand Lexicon Book'
to help you write your own Philosophy.

Finally, your Philosophy will tell you when
to say **Yes** or **No**.
The more freedom you have
the more you can use **Yes** or **No**.

"Philosophy is the highest music."   *Plato.*

***

~ ETHICS & MORALITY ~

Morality teaches us not to suffer and die,
but to enjoy ourselves and live.
Learning to take care of ourselves is a moral obligation.

Our brain is our computer,
our subconscious is our hard drive
and should be programed on an operating system
of Ethics and Morality.

You must build your Moral Character
by the choices you make based on your
Ethics, Morality and Philosophy.

It is hard to be Moral without Empathy, Gratitude.
Have the courage
to stop doing something immoral.
<u>You must not steal.</u>

"Character is that which reveals moral purpose."
Aristotle.

You must respect another person's property
and not wish to possess it.

Pay your bills on time.
<u>Never use profanity.</u>

NEVER CHEAT

**Being able to say <u>NO</u> is the essential element of
our moral compass and our integrity.**

Develop the moral skill to figure out
what is the right thing to do.

"Don't be penny wise and dollar foolish"

You must constantly remind yourself that a human life
cannot be replaced and consequently, you must regard
human life as precious.

You must want to be trustworthy, virtuous and sincere.

<u>Your reputation, dignity and character
are the most important things you have.</u>
<u>Ask do you like yourself? You can change.</u>

*"If I take care of my character,
my reputation will take care of itself."*
                    D.I.Moody.

"There are two races the decent man and the indecent man."
                    Denis Prager

People are good or evil.

Growing up you were molded by your parents, teachers,
peers and what you learned from others you believed in.
Their ethics and morality created a foundation
of knowledge and beliefs that until today
continue to influence the way you live.

If parents are moral and ethical,
in most cases their children will
lead a life based on ethics and morality.

No one has the right to do wrong even if wrong
has been done to them

When adults compromise ethically,
children will do the same while growing up
and continue to do so when they are adults.

The more people trust you,
the more your life will improve!

<u>Having morals and ethical friends is a must.</u>

Badness will rub of on you mixing with bad people.

Being honest gives you self-confidence and self-worth.

**<u>YOU BENEFIT ENORMOUSLY BY HAVING
ETHICAL MORALS AND VIRTUES.</u>**

**Morality is part of the blueprint to a happy life,
helping you make the right decisions,
upholding a standard of conduct
which will lead you to an uncomplicated,
joyful Happy life.**

Courage is needed to overcome adversity.

No society or person can grow without courage.

Nothing works well unless it is built
on a foundation of ethics and morals.
Just look at Governments, Industry and Marriage:
<u>all function badly when they don't have
Ethics and Morals as their foundation.</u>

Life is a lot simpler when people are honest.

<u>**You must treat people with respect.**</u>

We need to believe in truth.

*Moral character discloses a person's
deepest intentions towards you. Psychology Today.*

**The USA Constitution was made only for
people with morals,
and those who valued Freedom.**

**BEING GOOD AND MORAL
INCREASES YOUR HAPPINESS**

**HAPPY PEOPLE ENJOY LIFE
AND FIND LIFE IS EASIER BEING GOOD.
AND LIKE THEMSELVES.**

*"A man without ethics is a wild
beast loosed upon this world."
Albert Camus.*

*"To educate a person in the mind but not in morals
is to educate a menace to society." Theodore Roosevelt.*

"When people acquire good habits of character they are
better able to regulate their emotions and their reason.
This, in turn, helps us reach morally correct decisions
when we are faced with difficult choices."

"Goodness is about character, integrity, honesty,
kindness, generosity, moral courage, and the like.

*More than anything else,
it is about how we treat other people."
Dennis Prager.*

Always set a good and moral example.
***

◄COMMON MORALITY►

* Obey the law.
* Teach the young.
* Don't steal or cheat.
* Don't Kill or Disable.
* Respect others property.
* Do not commit adultery.
* Do not use verbal abuse.
* Don't use physical abuse.
* Don't punish the innocent.
* Rescue a person in danger.
* Tell the truth, do not deceive.
* Don't cause pain or suffering
* Don't mentally abuse anyone.
* Protect human life as precious.
* Honor your Father and Mother.
* Respect others and their views.
* Nurture the young and dependent.
* Don't deprive anyone of his or her freedom.
* Have good manners all the time and be polite.
* Don't deprive anyone of their pleasure and happiness.
* Always use moral considerations when dealing with people.
* Don't force or coerce anyone to do anything against their morals or will.

*   Log on to Prager University The Video about the
         Ten commandments is well worth looking at.
         www.prageruniversity.com/commandments.
                        ***

~ GOALS ~

**<u>The first goal on your list
should be your own happiness.
and a life well lived.</u>**

USE THE POWER OF YOUR BRAIN
TO ACHIEVE YOUR GOALS

Know what you want.

<u>Have realistic Goals.</u>

<u>Aim high but be reasonable about your Goal.</u>

You must be capable and have the necessary
attributes to get where you want to go.

For goals to work you have to own them.

Be disciplined.

Do not force goals on others.

Criticism, rejection should and must
put you back on the road to success.

You must have confidence, a clear vision
and a direct path to your goals.

**Sometimes you have to persevere
to reach your Goals.**

The reason for doing something should be
your driving force.

Passion often wins.

Enjoy the experience of getting to your goals.

Practice makes it easy.

Don't follow your dreams, follow your talent. Nell Scovell.

Most worth while Goals require effort
and a struggle to achieve.

Goals give you a road map to where you are going.
You will be lost if you don't know where
you want to go or what you want.

A Goal without a plan is just a wish.

Visualize and see yourself achieving your Goals.

Celebrate your improvement to your goals.

Remember Goals can be amended, changed
according to circumstances or postponed.

**It is important to clarify what is needed
in your life right now, and use your goals as a
reference in making decisions and choices.**

Accomplish something different every day.

*The key to achieving a goal is to **acknowledge
your fear or concern**, recognize the challenges ahead,
and frame your expectations in a manner
that creates an open path to success. Guy Winch. P.H.D.*

Long Term Goals can be achieved with a
combination of passion, perseverance and self control.

Because you have to devote more time to necessities,
balance long term goals with your life style.

*"Discipline is the bridge between
goals and accomplishment." Jim Rohn.*

Making things routine eliminates over thinking

Make things a routine to achieves your Goals.

Never let Fear interfere with your Goals.

***

OPTIMISM

Enjoy the now.

Being a optimist gives you a better chance to fight
disease and get <u>better health.</u>

Optimism is important in achieving your goals.

The good news is that if you are not an optimist
you can learn to be one.

*

Each day think about what you are grateful for,
make it a habit.

<u>Do not ever use the word **TRY;**</u>
<u>Always use the word **DO;**</u>
"I'm going to put in the Effort to **_DO_ _it!_** "

*"I am an optimist.
It does not seem to be
much use to be anything else."*
Winston S. Churchill.

"Choose to be optimistic, it feels better."
Dalai Lama XIV.

Be like some live a long and healthy life.

***

✶ HAPPINESS ✶

MUST BE BUILT ON A
FOUNDATION
OF
PHILOSOPHY, ETHICS, MORALITY
GOALS AND DISCIPLINE

Create conditions for happiness to occur.

*"MUCH OF WHAT DETERMINES OUR HAPPINESS IS
UNDER OUR CONTROL."*
Gary Small. M.D. U.C.L.A.

"Happiness is a moral obligation."
Dennis Prager.

If you read no further and set goals, have a
philosophy and ethics, and put purpose and meaning into your life,
you will be amazed how your life will improve quickly.

Happiness is a state of well being and containment.

**However reading the rest of this book will help you get
to your goals faster, because the rest of the book gives you
additional knowledge and reminders to help you achieve
success, happiness, a positive philosophy
for yourself and a much better life.**

Nature started us being happy that is our natural
state, some stay that way, others let the seeds of
unhappiness grow in them.

Nature has made man to be lazy, that is natural state
we have to fight nature by using **effort** so we are not lazy
and become a happy soul.

Happiness is having a happy disposition
lots of smiles laughter - love -
freedom -appreciation and a moral philosophy
Plus a best friend.

Joy adds to happiness.

Being happy makes you feel better,
it improves your health.
and helps you eat healthier,
and be more active, plus sleep better.

The book "Happiness is a serious problem"
written by Dennis Prager is well worth reading.

Happy people are great to be with.

Happy Quotes.

*"Happiness is not to be achieved at the command of emotional whims.
Happiness is not the satisfaction of whatever irrational wishes you
might blindly attempt to indulge."
"Happiness is a state of non-contradictory joy
without penalty of guilt.
It's joy that does not clash with any of your values
and does not work for your own destruction.
Its not the joy of escaping from your mind,
but using your mind's fullest power.
It's not the joy of faking reality, but achieving values that are real."*

*"Happiness is possible only to a rational man/women
It's possible for the man/women who desires nothing but
rational goals, seeks nothing but rational values
and finds their joy in nothing but rational actions."
"Happiness will only happen when we use our mind rationally."*
Ayn Rand.

*"Loss of values and meaning in life
make you unhappy.."*
Dennis Prager

*"Think! Grow prosperous.
Happiness is here and now. Stay grateful, stay present.
stay happy. Embrace life as it comes, embrace the moment.
We drift when we stop resisting."*
Katrina Izurieta.

WHAT IS HAPPINESS?

**A state of well being,
a feeling of inner joy, satisfaction and contentment.**
Having a calm joyful
peaceful state of mind, being grateful.

Happiness - 10% Genetic (Genes)
10% Circumstances, (How you were brought up etc.)

**YOUR HAPPINESS IS
<u>80% Under your control & the actions you choose.</u>**

YOUR HAPPINESS WILL ONLY HAPPEN
IF YOU USE YOUR BRAIN RATIONALLY.

HAPPINESS IS ENJOYING LIFE.

Your Happiness is being stable and persistent
<u>and having a meaningful life.</u>

Happiness is feeling good about yourself
without others approval.

*"Happiness is not having what you want,
but it is wanting what you have."*
Rabbi Hyman Schachtel.

Happiness comes to us in waves,
sometimes better than before, sometimes worse.

Your Happiness is your choice.

Freedom and gratitude
is very important for happiness.

Your Happiness doesn't just flow
from success it actually causes it.

Happiness grows brain cells, in the hippocampus,
about seven hundred new neurons per day.

"Happiness is the one thing obtainable by all free men.
We can get it by using our own brain and don't
need any special powers, genes or physical attributes
to achieve happiness." Ayn Rand.

"I will be happy until something awful happens."
Dennis Prager

"Happy people are more productive at work,
learn more in school, get promoted more,
are creative and are liked more."
Martin Seligman. Ph.D.

Don't talk yourself into believing your happy;
Be Happy.

Truth and evidence is hard to dispute.
NOW CHOOSE TO BE HAPPY.

WHY HAPPINESS

**Happiness is the most important reward
we give to ourselves.**

Happiness is within our reach and should be
our most important goal in life.

HAPPY PEOPLE HAVE MUCH LESS
STRESS AND SICKNESS.

Happy people are physically
healthier and live longer.

Happy people deal with adversity better.

<u>Your Happiness will attract the good things
in your life and bring you rewards.</u>

HAPPY PEOPLE LOVE LIFE.

Happy people live life more easily
than unhappy people do.

Happy people have good friends in their lives.

Happy people feel successful.

Happy people feel good.
Happy people are grateful, unhappy are not.

PURSUIT OF HAPPINESS

**The pursuit of happiness in America
is a fundamental right,
and the natural state of humanity.**

The question is are you pursuing happiness,
and putting sufficient effort in your life, -
work, - marriage, to be a happy soul?
Remember you control effort.
Sometimes we are better off making
changes to become a much happier person.

What gives each of us,
Pleasure and Happiness varies widely.
Some of us are living the life we are
supposed to, instead of the life we are mean't to.

To often we think I should do this, without
thinking will I be happy doing it.
Doing something because you want to,
makes one a lot happier, than doing something
because you should.

Focus what you are grateful for.

What matters in your life makes
a positive difference to happiness.
Do more of what makes you happy.
Having Best Friends increase your happiness.

HAPPINESS HAS NO LIMITS

**There are no limits on happiness except
for the limits we put on ourselves with our beliefs.**
Often we don't know how happy we are.

Happiness not only brings joy to the happy person,
it also is infectious to those who come in contact
with a happy person.

We want to be with happy people.

Happiness is taking responsibility, using intelligence in
a clear and coherent away.
Everything works better when you are happy.

Living a life you choose will bring you happiness.

You don't need any special physical or mental attributes
acquired through others to obtain happiness.
You are in tune with yourself.

"Happiness depends upon ourselves." Aristotle.

Happiness is pleasure plus meaning
and mental engagement.

Repeat often "I choose to be happy."
Be Happy & Smile!

CHOOSE TO BE HAPPY
That is the only way to find happiness.

Remember happy people **choose** to be happy.

<u>Happiness is a choice we make in life,
some people choose to be unhappy.</u>

Happy people love life.
Happy people know a good thing when they see it.

Happy people look good, walk relaxed,
smile a lot, and use words like-
Change! - Thinking!
Grateful! - Happy! - Pleased!
Wonderful! - Brilliant! - Marvelous! - Sensational
- Excellent! - Outstanding! - Superb! - Super!
First rate! - Great! - Fantastic
Love - Like - Fond

*" I, not events, have the power to make me happy or
unhappy today. I can choose which it shall be.
Yesterday is dead, tomorrow hasn't arrived yet.
I have just one day, today, and I'm going to be happy in it."*
Groucho Marx.

No one has the power to make you unhappy,
unless you let them.
You have to use courage to be strong.
You have the power to make yourself happy or unhappy.

TO ACHIEVE HAPPINESS YOU HAVE TO HAVE SOME OF THE FOLLOWING……

Good health. Love.
Perseverance. Goals.
Passion. Enthusiasm Being grateful.

High Self-Esteem and Self-Worth.
Self-Assurance.
Satisfaction with your life.
Freedom & Independence.
Enthusiasm. Good Values.
You must be able to celebrate Life.
Always expect to be happy.

You must be passionate about everything you do
and have friends who share your values and morals.

Bring smiles to others.
It is important to have happy people in your life
and those who support you.
Develop a satisfying social network with good
conversations showing respect, appreciation, and laughter.

Happiness <u>requires effort;</u>
you <u>don't need </u>any effort to be unhappy.
The more effort you put in the better is the result.

Build on your strength.
Be kind to people. Commit acts of kindness.

Count your blessings and be grateful.

Practical wisdom is one of the keys to happiness.
You must live according to your values.

<u>Your career must have a productive purpose,
a conscious, rational pursuit and be productive.</u>

To achieve happiness you
have to <u>discipline</u> yourself to do well,
be optimistic and deal with stress positively.

YOU CAN CHOOSE TO BE HAPPY OR UNHAPPY.

You must have something to look forward to.

<u>Exercise,</u> is a must, take a walk, eat healthily,
do mindful meditation and affirmations.

You must have:
Confidence in yourself and be self-reliant, have
achievements, satisfaction and appreciation in your life.
and like yourself.
Have a sense of humor.
Look at the funny side of life and disregard envious or
jealous thoughts. Find the humor in the negative,
not forgetting to add fun to passion and you will
reach excellence and happiness quickly.
Be tactful! Being tactful does not mean agreement,
it is not stressing your success or happiness
in the presence of those who are suffering.

WHAT IMPEDES HAPPINESS

Low Self-Esteem / Low Self-Worth.
Complaining instead of making changes.

<u>Not enough laughter in your life.</u>
(Laughter can jolt the immune system into gear,
opens the door to happiness.)

<u>Insufficient Funds</u>
Buying things on credit and not being able to pay for them
at the end of the month and paying high interest fees.

Buying to impress others.

Too many negative emotions, thoughts and events.
Thinking about the unpleasant past.

Not disciplining yourself to accept reality.
Lack of maturity and discipline when you don't win
or get what you want.

Not learning from your mistakes.

<u>Being a victim makes you unhappy.</u>

<u>Also Associating with unhappy or immoral people.</u>

Fear will make you unhappy.
<u>Don't let fear rule your life.</u>

What is substance abuse?
Substance abuse is trying to negate unhappiness sadness,
and that which may be in the conscious or subconscious
mind with foreign substances, you put in your body.

You must admit to yourself you have a problem
when you are trying to get high,
<u>you must seek help.</u>

Get high on life is a better way to be happy.

**Happiness should not depend
on instant Gratification.**

The following impede happiness.
Lack of Love.
Lack of appreciation and gratitude.
Lack of spontaneity in one's life.
Lack of a new event in a persons life.
Lack of adventures.
Lack of wisdom. <u>Not learning.</u>
Not having a life companion to share with.
Not having a very best friend.
People in your life who affect you negatively.
Friends who's morals and ethics
are not as good as yours.
Being a boring person. Being bored.
You must not sit on the couch too long.
To much T.V. or use of phones.

**Don't join groups whose purpose is to change
you to their philosophy and at the same time ask
you to part with your money, with the hope
you will be rewarded for giving.**
You will be associating
with unhappy, depressed people.

Buyer beware.

Using power over others or the lack of power
will have a negative effect on your happiness.

**You will not be happy with work
you do not enjoy or working with people
you do not get along with or like.**

Putting all your faith in experts, comparing
yourself to others will make you unhappy.

Not being self sufficient will impede you.

If you have an inferiority complex, or other
complexes about yourself or your physical
appearance you should seek professional help.

You must concentrate on improving
your personality: the essence of who you are
is far more important
than your physical appearance.

<u>Harboring envious and jealous thoughts
is very damaging to you and others.</u>

*"Be aware that negative expectation of yourself and
others are likely to produce negative results."*
Pierce J Howard. Ph.D.

<u>We usually get in the way of our own happiness.</u>

"Ingratitude leads to unhappiness."   Dennis Prager.

*Remember: "Things are almost never as bad -
or as good - as we expect them to be." Daniel Gilbert.*

**Not choosing a proper diet
will effect your happiness and moods.**
A Mediterranean Diet or Keto seems to be the best.

You happiness should not be
at the expense of others.

Depression - Obesity -
Stress - Argument - Addictions - Drugs Alcohol.
all impede happiness.

Lies people tell you will impede your happiness.
Also unfulfilled promises.
Narcissistic friends will hurt you in every way possible.

"Let your hope, not your hurts, shape your future."
Robert H. Schuller.

Addictions produce Dopamine in the Brain.
Dopamine give one a pleasure response.
The life of a addict is lonely empty and unfulfilling
Only Action can make changes.

"A remark generally hurts in proportion to its truth."
Will Rogers.

"Beware of Destination Addiction,
such as; the idea that happiness is in the next place,
next job or with the next partner.
Until you give up the idea that it is somewhere else
it will never be where you are."
Robert Holden. P.h.D. Psychologist.

"You won't find happiness from mysticism.
John Zizzo P.hD.

Some Websites manipulate the brain
to produce Dopamine
to get you addicted to their website.
Be aware you are being manipulated
don't let these Websites get their way.

Being negative is detrimental to happiness.

Use Moderation to avoid being unhappy.
in everything you do.

HAPPY PEOPLE

Happy people choose to be happy.
<u>Happiness is a choice we make in life,</u>
<u>some people choose to be unhappy.</u>

Happy people love life.
Happy people know a good thing when they see it.
Happy people look good, walk relaxed,
smile a lot, and use words like:
Change - Thinking -
Grateful - Happy - Pleased -
Wonderful! - Marvelous! - Sensational! -
Excellent! - Outstanding! - Superb! - Super!-
First rate! - Great! - Fantastic! - Brilliant!
Love - Like - Fond

Happy people look younger than their age.

Happy people are contented people.
Happy people add color to their lives.

Happy people find enjoyment in
simple and complex situations and things.

Happy have no trouble attracting the opposite sex.

**Happy people turn their mistakes
into learning and curiosity.**

Happy people love to learn.

Happy people are **achievers.**

Happy people do not gossip;
they speak well of people.

Happy people don't argue.

Happy people recognize evil.

Happy people like to dance.

Happy people treat people nicely.

Happy people make you feel good.

Happy people have a zest for living.

Happy people love to help people and teach.

Happy people have good friends in their lives.

Happy people love to give good advice when asked.

Happy people feel successful and are successful.

Happy people turn problems into opportunities.

**HAPPY PEOPLE OFTEN FORGET TIME
AND ARE IN THE FLOW THESE MOMENTS ARE
FUN AND VERY SPECIAL TO HAPPY PEOPLE.**

*"I will never understand all the good that a simple
smile can accomplish."*
Mother Teresa.

HAPPY PEOPLE APPRECIATE THE
GOOD THINGS IN THEIR LIVES
AND ARE GRATEFUL.
IT MAKES THEM FEEL GOOD.

Happy people care about their work, their customers,
people around them and people they love and like.

Happy people are grateful for things
that others take for granted.

Happy people spend less time frustrating themselves
about grey areas and concentrate their time
and effort on black and white areas.

Happy people are enthusiastic,
persevering, curious and quietly aggressive.

Happy people spend more money on experiences,
such as doing something with others, learning, going
to concerts etc.and less time on material things.

**Happy people are creative and
make items or sell items that benefit others.
They like to give good service and give pleasure.**

Happy people are comfortable with their unique identity
and see happiness their way.

Happy people do charity work or help someone in need.

Happy people don't *have* the best
of everything; they *make* the best of everything.

Happiness is the art of never holding
in your mind negative thoughts.

Expectations can lead to disappointments.

Appreciation leads to happiness.

*"Twenty years from now you will be more disappointed by
the things that you didn't do, than by the one's you did do.
So throw off the bow lines, sail away from the safe harbor
catch the trade winds and sale, explore, dream, discover."*
Mark Twain.

Happy people smile a lot.

Happy people even smile and
laugh when they are alone.

HAPPINESS & PLEASURE

IMPORTANT
Ask yourself: will it give me happiness
or pleasure?

Pleasure a feeling of happy satisfaction
and enjoyment.

Happiness that depends mainly on physical
pleasure is unstable because one day it is there,
the next day it may not be there.

True happiness relates more
to the mind and heart.

Money will not purchase happiness for you
if you have no concept of what you want:
money will not give you a code of values.

Money will not give you happiness if you
evaded the knowledge of what to value;
money will not and should not provide
you a purpose in your life.

Money does make you more comfortable
when used correctly.

Money does free you from financial worries.

**Money does give you the opportunity to be
more free and independent.**

Money will make you feel good,
helping those in need.

*"The noblest pleasure is
the joy of understanding."*
Leonardo da Vinci.

*"Pleasure in the job puts
perfection in the work."*

*"The aim of the wise is not to
secure pleasure but to
avoid pain."*
Aristotle.

*"Pleasure and action make
the hours seem short."*
William Shakespeare.

*"Money will not buy intelligence for the fool,
or admiration for the coward or
respect for the incompetent."*
Ayn Rand.

Machines - Computers -I Phones can give you
pleasure - only humans can give you **true love**.
***

DON'T FORGET

**After you have sufficient money
to live at a good standard of living
and your needs are met,
making more money
will not bring you more happiness.**

Be productive.

Your employer must make money on you or
you will loose your job.

Once you clarify your philosophy,
ethics, morality and goals,
everything in your life will start to work
the way you want.
You will be using the power of your brain.
You will start to live your life to the fullest.

After clarifying your life, your meaning and
<u>purpose for living,</u> you will find yourself
seeking information that you can use
to bring more happiness into your life.

Your brain will be actively involved in using reason
to make necessary changes to reach your goals.
You will be seeking activities that bring you
happiness and finding ways
to avoid doing mundane things.

**Making decisions is so much easier
when you base it on your Happiness,
Philosophy, Morality and Goals.
Good Values**
You missed opportunities in the past,
<u>have no regrets;</u>
because opportunities never stop coming.
Learn from the past to recognize opportunities;
this time grab the opportunity as it avails itself to you.

You must consider making big
and small changes in your life and be motivated
to put them into practice to achieve your goals.

You must always learn and put learning to good use.

<u>Your life must have a purpose and meaning
your happiness.</u>

*"People say money is not the key to happiness
but I always figured if you had enough money,
you can have a key made."*

*"ALWAYS CARRY A SENSE OF HUMOR
Wit takes you from victim to victor over life's ugliness."*
Regina Barreca.
Happiness is a choice.

Laugh!
Smile!

IT IS NEVER TOO LATE TO INCREASE YOUR HAPPINESS

HOW DO YOU KNOW YOU ARE HAPPY?
If you smile when you are alone.
If you can get up every day think or say:
"I AM HAPPY TO BE ALIVE!
I FEEL WONDERFUL!"

ASK YOUR SELF ARE YOU:
Very unhappy
Unhappy
Zero happy
or
Happy
Very Happy
Extremely Happy.
∧

Which one are you?

~ ~ ~

Next is Self-Esteem, Reason, Purpose,
they are the three things we must hold as the
supreme ruling values of our lives.
***

HABITS

**We develop good and bad habits
during our life time.**
We start life with few habits.

Often the secret of success is found in
in your daily routine and habits.

*"We are what we repeatedly do.
Excellence, then, is not an act, but a habit."* Aristotle.

**Make it a habit to compliment everyone you meet,
especially friends and people you love,
it will pay off in many ways. Be truthful.**

To eliminate bad habits **brain wash** yourself by
saying to yourself every hour
you are a awake…. I must not do (name the habit)
any more. (See Affirmations page 197)

To get good habits also **brain wash** yourself by
saying to yourself every hour
you are a wake for three days, I must do…
(name the habit) every day.

*"The most important thing you can do for yourself
is to avoid having negative behaviors and harmful habits.*
Dr.T.P. Chia.

***

SELF- ESTEEM / SELF WORTH

**Self-Esteem is reliance on one's power to think,
knowing our mind is competent,
worthy of happiness.**

People with high Self-Esteem
do well in relationships.

Self-esteem / Self-Worth empowers us to learn
and makes it easy to do things.
Self-esteem is earned.
Self-Confidence represents good judgment.
Don't confuse Self-Confidence with Self-Esteem.

Thinking positively about a situation
in which the odds of success
are exceedingly low may not be realistic.
Don't be a highly enthusiastic incompetent.
Knowing one's limitations may be even more
important than knowing one's talents.
We all have strengths others don't have.
A person with low Self-Esteem is
more vulnerable to stress.

*"Look in the mirror; notice the way you like
yourself, will be the way you treat yourself and others.
Say to the mirror* **"I like you, I really like you."**
Do this often to make it work.

**IT IS EASY TO JUDGE THE MISTAKES
OF OTHERS
BUT DIFFICULT TO RECOGNIZE
OUR OWN MISTAKES.**
<u>Know who you are,</u>
<u>ask your best friend for feedback</u>
<u>and the truth as they see you.</u>
You can't read people's minds
and know what they think about you;
do not assume you know.

You must be able to write and speak well.

*"The worst loneliness is to not be
comfortable with yourself." Mark Twain.*

*"Believe in yourself! Have faith in your
abilities! Without a humble but reasonable
confidence in your own powers you cannot
be successful or happy." Norman Vincent Peale.*

*"No one can make you feel inferior
without your consent." Eleanor lRoosevelt.*

Focus on your good qualities.
Like yourself - Take care of yourself.
Remember; people don't notice you,
as much as you may believe.
"Variety is the spice of life."
****

~ REASON ~

Reason is our tool of knowledge.
When you use the power of reasoning you find and integrate
the material from your senses. (Neurons.)
Don't buy the first thought that comes into
your head use Reason, Knowledge, Good Judgement
Common Sense, Wisdom.
Knowledge truth and facts, helps you reason,

$$A = A$$

~

You may have to reprogram your brain
with knowledge, truths, fact and positive information,
so that when you use the power of reason you will
make the right decisions and choices.

Reason is the capacity for consciously and
intuitively making sense of things, applying logic,
establishing and verifying facts and changing
or justifying practices, belief based on
new or existing information.
Be open to revising your thinking.
Wishful thinking; may be just a wish and not be true.

"Reason and judgement are the qualities of a leader." Tacitus.

"How we act is far more important than how we think or feel."
Don't generalize give examples. Dennis Prager.
***

TIME
**Do not waste each day;
every night critique the day,
rejoice if it went well.**

Utilize your time for your benefit and love one's.

<u>Manufacture time by being more efficient.</u>
Turn of your smart phone to create more time.
Use your time for your priorities.

Boredom <u>can</u> make us do
interesting things **<u>if we let it.</u>**

*"The time you <u>enjoy</u>
wasting is not wasted time."*
Bertrand Russell.

*"Slow down and enjoy life,
Its not only the scenery you miss by going
to fast - you also miss the sense of where
you are going and why."* *Eddie Cantor.*

*"What dog can tell the time?
A watch dog."*

Smile !
**

~ PURPOSE ~

Purpose tells us what is important, what is meaningful.
Productive creative work should be one of the
purposes of your life and **your happiness.**

Clarity of purpose, prioritizing, resisting impulses
and a sense of mission will lead to great results.
Habit gets things done if you let it become routine.
Pick a set of high-value activities as part of your strategy.

A person without purpose is lost in chaos drifting at the
mercy of chance, searching for value he will never find.
Ask yourself what is my purpose in life?

"The secret of success is constancy of purpose." Disraeli.

Unlock your Purpose for living, choose and make your life
as it should be. Say "Yes to life." "Be Happier." Be curious.

Reflect why you were born, this should give
you a sense of purpose and a meaning for living.
Fulfill what you are mean't to do.
Helping others gives one purpose.
*"Deep boredom of the soul, is the boredom than emanates
from lack of purpose and a yearning for excitement."*
Dennis Prager
Live as if you were living already for the second time and
and as if you had acted the first time wrongly correct it now.
***

FREEDOM

**Freedom is one of he most important
and precious things.**

We must never take freedom for granted.

When you loose your freedom
you loose your soul to those
who took your freedom away.

You must have freedom
to choose to say **NO.**

You must say **NO**
to protect your freedom when necessary.

If you are married or single, freedom has to be
of paramount importance in your relationships,
your life and your philosophy.

Do not let anyone take your freedom away by
<u>coercing you into doing anything</u>
<u>against your will or your morals.</u>

A person or a employer who uses his money
to coerce you to his will, or does not understand
you when you refuse to obey, is not the
right person in your life.

Having freedom
is very important in life.

**Money often lets you have more freedom
and should not be taken for granted.**

Money lets you pay others to do work you
might normally do, so you have time to
do things you enjoy doing.

Money lets you manage your time better.
Money gives you the ability to help others.

"Man is free at the moment he wishes to be."
Voltaire.

*"Those who deny freedom to others,
deserve it not for themselves."*
Abraham Lincoln.

*"Far greater than all the material possessions
that we possess is our freedom to choose our friends
and loved one's and our freedom to be happy"*
Unknown Author.

*We must have freedom to choose to be happy.
"It is the spiritual freedom which cannot be taken away -
that makes life meaningful and purposeful." Victor E Frankel.*
*****

TRUTH

TRUTH IS REALITY - REALITY IS TRUTH
Truth is that which never changes.
Each truth is better than the one before.

*"What can be asserted without proof
can be dismissed without proof."*
Christopher Hitchens.

HONESTY IS THE BEST POLICY.

Always tell the truth;
it is the easiest thing to remember.
No legacy is so rich as honesty.

You may not wan't to hurt someones feelings
by telling the truth, but remember this may
have unintended consequences later
when the truth is exposed.

*"The truth doesn't cost you anything but
a lie could cost you everything."* Unknown

<u>Some people believe their own lies.</u>

"Intellect will bring you the truth." Sasha.

*"Be true to your own world and you're automatically
in others' world, too."* Rene Clement. Film maker.

**The truth may hurt for a little while
but a lie hurts forever.**

Do not be gullible.
If it sounds to good to be true, it probably isn't true.
When in doubt check it out use common sense.

You can be mistaken or misled at any given time.
You must be inflexible in regard to seeking
and demanding the truth.

A lie is an intentional false statement;
don't confuse it with being mistaken
which is coming to a wrong conclusion.

Many people like to exaggerate and
lie about their accomplishments;
some even pretend to be what they are not.
Others just lie to get you to do their bidding
and make false promises.
Remember actions speak louder than words.
Judge people by their actions.
Always keep an open mind.

Some men indulge in putting you on;
they believe it is humorous to lie;
they do not believe they are lying as they
believe you do not believe them anyway.
Con men are very accomplished at telling lies.
***

PLACEBO EFFECT

Some people experience a benefit from the placebo effect.
The brain reacts to a placebo; a fake stimulus,
and makes the body react often for our benefit.

Our belief system, how we think and believe
is a very powerful tool; us it wisely,
for your benefit and for mental and body health.
We live longer if we think we will.
We are a lot happier if we believe we are a happy person.

Prayer, meditation can improve ones health and well being;
due to the placebo effect it has on our brain.

We can also use our belief system to our detriment;
by thinking negative thoughts and beliefs.
<u>Beliefs have to be truthful and factual.</u>
If we believe we are unhappy we will be.

Happiness is a choice we make, the placebo effect,
can make us happy and in a good mood.

Thinking positive is very powerful force
in making good choices for ourselves.

Get up in the morning and tell yourself you will be;
"very happy to day".
works like magic.
***

~ THE BRAIN ~

**Your brain is the most powerful tool you own;
use it or lose it.**

Shape the mind.
Challenges makes the brain more efficient.

Take control of your brain.

You must think positively to make the brain work well.
Keep a positive outlook.

"You are not your brain, you are the user of your brain."
Dr. Rudy Tanz.

Make good choices.

Learning something new every day, improves the mind.
Learning protects newly formed brain cells.

TRAIN THE BRAIN.

Beliefs are created as a reflex.

"The energy of the mind is the essence of life."
Aristotle.

Your brain has the power to reason,
learn and be more resilient.

PAY ATTENTION - FOCUS - LISTEN - SEE - HEAR.

Doing new activities is great for
the brain and ones well being.

*"The mind is its own place and in itself can make
a Heav'n of Hell, or a Hell of Heav'n."*
John Milton.

*"The brain can't tell emotional the difference looking at
a movie, or reading a book, it reacts the same way."*
David Eagleman. P.B.S

The brain has limited capacity to store
information short term (About seven items)
after which it goes to long-term memory.

The brain has quadrillion different connections,
which makes each person a unique individual.

Your brain is like a computer programmed
during the first years of your life by your parents,
teachers and peer groups.

You now have the opportunity to reprogram
yourself to achieve your goals
and improve your wellbeing.

Capitalize on your brain's strengths.
Part of your brain stores information that becomes
the essence of your personality.

**Not everyone's brain develops the same way,
for example: one brain might be better
at math, another at art.
Learn your strengths.**

Your childhood experiences, based on knowledge
you acquired throughout the years, combined with
your genes, greatly influence
how you use your brain today.

A record of one's actions, morals and ethics
are memorized
in the subconscious part of the brain.
Get rid of the clutter in your brain,
organize your brain.

Change negative thought by thinking about a
wonderful, joyful time in your life
or a beautiful landscape or sunset.
Do this as often as you can.

Don't let Emotions:
Aggressiveness - Negative thoughts
dominate your brain.
Keep a well-balanced brain.

*"When you're born, you make feelings like calmness
and agitation, excitement, comfort, discomfort.
These simple feelings are not emotions.
They are summaries of what is going on
in your body, kind of like a barometer." Lisa F Barrett. Ph.D.*

Accept reality… be practical.
It takes courage to look at reality in ones life,
and accept it and not try to change it.

It takes courage to stand on principle.

You must master and control your brain.

Coaches make star Athletes
say over and over they will win.
Repeating concepts over and
over trains the brain.

Say twenty times "I won't smoke any more!"
as often as you can for three days
and you will not want to smoke anymore.

It's important use your brain to find out the truth.

"The quality of our brain's output, like a computer,
is determined by the quality of input.
If the subconscious is programmed by chance,
our brain's output will react accordingly." Ayn Rand.

Our subconscious does not know
what is real or imagined.

Tap into the power of your brain.
Remember the brain can't
multitask efficiently.

**The more you learn how the brain works,
the more efficiently you can use your brain,
leading you to a better life.**

Driving and talking on the phone
is like driving under the influence.
Don't risk getting into a accident.

**For better memory, pay attention, focus.
<u>Mindful Meditation</u> & Affirmations will train
you to focus and is a must to keep the brain healthy.**

Thinking and concentrating on what you are
doing, will often make the act more enjoyable.
Example:
Thinking about the taste of the food,
while you eat and not talking will make
eating more enjoyable,
providing the food is pleasant to eat.

THE BRAIN NEEDS
8 hours sleep nightly
<u>this a must for a healthy brain.</u>
Walking and Vitamin D, Exercise, enhance the brain.

A happy brain works much better
than a brain plagued by unhappiness.

The brain likes hobbies.

**Thinking about two items reinforces
short-term memory in the brain.**
Example: When you put your KEYS down think about
the object you put your KEYS on, such as a TABLE.
The two items to remember are KEYS & TABLE.
Now you won't forget where your keys are;
always use this concept to remember important things.

Good Close Relationships protects Brain Cells.
The brain needs people Friends.

*Your neurons depend on other people's neurons.
Social network, friends, are vital for our survival.
We are hardwired to be social creatures."*
David Eagleman. P.BS.

"Tears come from the heart and not from the brain."
Leonardo da Vinci.

Be careful, your imagination can mislead you
when thinking about the future or the past.
You brain has the ability to imagine episodes
that never happened in your past
You only remember fragments of what happened
in the past; your brain fills in what is missing
from what it knows now.

The brain is easily tricked.

Magicians know how to trick you.

<u>Con Men, Cult Leaders, Narcissists & </u>Others
know how to <u>manipulate your brain </u>into
believing things, which are not factual.

The brain does not always know what it wants,
it only knows what it knows.

Puzzles, Meditation, **Exercise,** Creativity,
Naps, Learning, Reading, Writing, Happiness,
Laughter, Vitamins, Vegetables,
all are good for the brain.

Stress shrinks the brain

We have the power to change our brain every day.

The brain is plastic and changes by experience.
Learning, focusing, paying attention,
makes the brain more efficient.

Challenge yourself on a daily basis,
to improve the brains performance.
We can fine tune our brain to be more efficient.
How the neurons connect to each other by electric
impulses speeds up with how we fine tune our brain.
The brain is like a orchestra, each instrument (neurons),
works in concert.

To work efficiently the brain needs you
to do everything in moderation.

Training the brain can bring it back to normality.

Calibrate the brains irregularities yourself -
know where you have to improve.

Whats good for your body
is good for your brain.

What you eat is very important
for the Brain to function well.

The brain controls your good health.

Learning new skills and **exercise,**
focusing on a challenge is excellent for the brain.

Focus your attention - pay attention - all the time.

*Problem solving and dealing with adversities in life is good
for the brain, it creates new neurons and connections.*

*Good deeds helps your brain - good social connections,
(friendship) helps the brain.*

*Train your brain and change your
life for the better is very important.
www.BrainHQ.com - Dr. Merzenich*
***

INTELLIGENCE - KNOWLEDGE

**Intelligence is quickness of understanding,
a rational being who has wisdom and is
discerning has retrieval and relevance.**

KNOWLEDGE BUILDS ON KNOWLEDGE.
We humans have a great need to know.

Intelligence is the ability to understand knowledge
and put it to good use to benefit oneself.
Hardships can be avoided by learning what to do.

Intelligence is the ability to make **good decisions**
and **good choices** to analyze and make
judgements based on facts.
Intelligence helps us make conscientious decisions
and **moral choices** to pursue happiness and to set goals.

Knowledge derives from pure reasoning.
Listening and studying both sides of a argument.
Knowledge is power if we use knowledge wisely.
We must constantly expand our knowledge.

Put knowledge you have learned to work
for your benefit and others.

Intelligence is the ability to go beyond
where you are now.
***

EDUCATION
<u>Learn something new every day.</u>

<u>Be defined by your curiosity
and thirst for learning.</u>

You learn while you listen.
Make notes of important items
you don't want to forget.

Life is always teaching us a lesson;
we have to pay attention and learn
from these lessons and from mistakes.

*"To be educated is in fact to be able to do this.
That is, a person can only claim to be educated
if he able to be critical, <u>if he is able to distinguish
between sense and nonsense</u> even when he is not
a specialist in any one are of knowledge, to be able to
distinguish between the truth and lies."*

*"Education is the best provision
for the journey to old age." Aristotle.*

*"Imagination is more important than knowledge,
The value of education is not the learning of
many facts but the training of the mind to think." Albert Einstein*

Prager University is a <u>great easy place to learn.</u>
****

WISDOM

"*Life is simple book*" is filled with wisdom.
Wisdom is asking what is good.
You must strive in life to have quality experiences.

You must make good judgements and be wise.

Your actions must be based on your philosophy,
morals, ethics, purpose, goals,
experiences, knowledge and good judgement.

Wisdom is being aware of
the unintended consequences from actions.

Wisdom is made not born.
Wisdom comes from experience.
Knowledge speaks, wisdom listens.

Our belief system makes us act.
Sometimes what we believe is wrong.
Wisdom and knowledge, learning ,
experience and wise people
corrects us when we are wrong.

Wisdom makes us weigh our beliefs correctly.

"Its not enough to be nice, you need wisdom."
Wisdom asks what are the consequences?
DenissPrager

**Wisdom is the ability to make sound judgements
based on experience and knowledge and beliefs.**

Always reflect thoughtfully on experience.
Think about both sides, weigh the pros and the cons.

Without Wisdom you are a foolish person.
If you add thought and wisdom
you become a wise person.

*"Wisdom lies in acting on the world as it is,
not as we wish it to be." Jena Pincott.*

"Wisdom is learning from others."
"Wisdom is every thing" Dennis Prager.

*"Wisdom is not a product of schooling but
of the lifelong attempt to acquire it." Albert Einstein.*

"Knowing yourself is the beginning of all wisdom."
Aristotle.

*"To know what you know and
to know what you don't know
that is real wisdom." Confucius*

**Important
Know your strength and weakness.
One must confront reality in order to grow.**
***

HOW TO THINK

Take the time to think.

"Change your thought and you change your world."
Norman Vincent Peal.

Always look for simple solutions.

Focusing while thinking enhances awareness.

Learn to focus on solutions not on problems.

"I ask people what it is they want
and you would be amazed at how few of them know;
if you focus on what you want, things clear up."
Oprah Winfrey.

The best way to get something done is to start.
Just do it! don't think about it and procrastinate.

Knowledge tell's you what works best for you,
until you learn that another solution
might be proven better.

Achievements are rewards to you and others.
In all your actions you must strive for excellence.
<u>Remember always ask is that the best you can do?</u>

Focus on what you do best.

71

Meaning well therefor I am doing good,
can often lead to a bad outcome

You must not be affected by
negativity around you.

Talk to yourself positively.
Think for yourself. - Be individualistic.
<u>You must be able to say **NO**.</u>

People say offensive things.
<u>Their remarks cannot harm</u>
<u>you unless you permit it.</u>

Don't assume you are always right.

What others say is right for you
should never make you feel guilty if you don't agree.

Our nature is judgmental replace it with curiosity.

You must take control of your life.

You must not be frustrated when
your best is not good enough.

Don't be afraid to seek and ask for help.
You must know when you need to ask for help.

You must not let yourself suffer from anxiety.

**Compounding your growth one percent
will have spectacular results.**

You have to be enthusiastic,
persevering and quietly aggressive.
Laziness impedes productivity.

Talk less and say more.
You must stimulate your imagination and creativity.
Don't climb over the mountain unless you
have a love of mountain climbing.Take the easy route.
Challenge yourself with things you like to do.
You should learn from other
people's experiences and books.
You must ask yourself:
does what I am doing add value to my life?
When you are looking for answers, step back
and look at the whole picture unemotionally.
Ask yourself, what can I do to improve today?

When life is not working change yourself,
change the situation.
Know what you can control and what you can't.
A wise person knows how to improvise.

"Don't focus on what is missing in your life." Dennis Prager.

You look at a play or film to be entertained; now start
looking at real life the same way, there is plenty to laugh at.
***

PROCRASTINATION

Procrastination is our struggle with self control,
hidden fears, avoiding difficult tasks deliberately
looking for distractions over our goals.

*"Cultivate a realistic optimistic outlook by
combining confidence in your ability to succeed
with an honest assessment of the challenges
that await you. Don't visualize success -
visualize the steps and obstacles you
will have take in order to make success happen."*
Heidi G.Halvorson. Ph.D.

Be realistic use honest assessment of your
abilities use reason to accomplish your goals.

Visualization is a must for Athletes.
The more you imagine yourself in the future the more
emotionally connected you feel to that future self.
Say to yourself -
This is not my favorite task but I can do it.
Break the task up into smaller portions.
Get a partner to help you.
Reward your accomplishments.
Be realistic. Don't be a perfectionist.
Ask - What will make it worth while?

"Procrastination is the thief of time." Edward Young.
***

EMOTIONS

"Emotions are guesses - predictions."

"Emotions are billions of our brain cells (neurons), firing like mad,
working together, trying to make sense of millions of our experiences
over a lifetime weighing the probabilities, trying to answer, guessing;
'What is this most like' - 'not what is it.'
the brains sifts thru past experiences and comes up
with an emotional answer.
Emotions are not built into our brain at birth.
Predictions are basically the way your brain works.
Predictions are the basis of every experience,
they are the basis of every action we take.
Predictions make us understand conversations.
Predictions help us make sense of the world,
using past experiences, the brain constructs
our experience of the world."
Lisa F Barrett. Ph.D.

"Don't be a prisoner of your emotions." Dennis Prager.

When you are Emotional you are vulnerable.
Don't let emotions take over use **Reason** take action.

Emotions are not reality.
We are nothing without Emotions.

Emotions can drive us wrongly, so be careful.
Try not to argue, control your emotions.

You must prioritize emotional health.

Calmness, agitation, excitement,
comfort, discomfort etc. - are not emotions,
they are simple feelings that come, when we
are born from physiology of our body.

*"Feelings of spirituality are a matter of emotions
rather than intellect."*
Pierce J Howard. Ph.D.

Our emotions are:
anger, fear, disgust, happiness, sadness,
excitement, disgust, horror, anxiety, envy, shame,
relief, surprise, pain, confusion, awkwardness, boredom,
craving, entrancement, awe, aesthetic appreciation,
admiration, joy, sexual desire, lust, adoration, amusement.

Emotions control our thinking,
behavior and actions.
Your emotions must not be contrary to your
Morality, Philosophy, Goals and Purpose.

Emotions indicate negatives against positives
and gives us an estimate of values for us or against us;
they give us instantly: our profit and loss.
A clever person discovers the source of his emotions
and how he got the premise and correct it if it is wrong.
A clever person never acts on an emotion
he does not understand.

Don't make judgments emotionally.
Manage your emotions.
Do not ignore your Emotions.
Your feelings can make you choose badly.
You are better off using your brain than your gut feelings
when your subconscious is, programmed incorrectly.

Emotions tell you how you value reality.
Have a healthy understanding of your emotions.

Don't take on others emotional pain;
Give sympathy not empathy.
Take care of yourself so you can help others.
Ask yourself what do you fear.

Mindful Meditation, Yoga, Exercise,
Healthy Eating is good for your Emotions.

"Worry never robs tomorrow of its sorrow;
it only sap today of its strengths." A.J.Cronin.

Emotions can affect your physical body,
make you ill and negative and lead to helplessness.
Being rejected is painful, and can make one
tell oneself, things that are hurtful.
Learn that rejection is part of living.

Lack of appreciation gives us a bad feeling.

The only person who can change how you feel is you.

<u>You must be able to say NO.</u>
Do you believe your Emotions?

Anger is a reflex preventing one's self being exploited;
it's a way of getting attention to get one's point across.

**<u>A MEASURED RESPONSE WITH CONFIDENCE
AND EMPHASIS IS BETTER THAN ANGER.</u>**
Expressing genuine emotions and standing
one's ground are valuable skills, in love and work.

<u>Bad temper and extreme anger</u>
are very destructive and can effect one's health,
<u>Professional help is needed.</u>

Positive emotions can be justified.
Negative emotions can't be justified.
Express yourself carefully and unemotional.
YOU MUST STOP EMOTIONAL BLEEDING.
Talking honestly to a friend helps
Don't let fear of disappointing oneself or others -
by failing to meet a wanted goal, stop you moving ahead.
<u>IMPORTANT</u>
In this day and age we hear a lot of name
calling in the media, schools, and at home,
don't let this or your emotions distress you.

Remember: *"Sticks and stones can break my bones
but names can never hurt me."*
***

HOW TO THINK CRITICALLY

**Critical thinking is the process of analysis and
assessing claims and making judgments
on the basis of well-supported evidence.**

What am I being asked to believe or accept?
What evidence is available to support the assertion?
Are there alternative ways of interpreting the evidence?
What conclusions are most reasonable?

Observe yourself objectively.
Don't get to attached to your opinions test
them against criticism.

"The important thing is never stop questioning." Albert Einstein.

*"Thinking for yourself or others will think for you
without thinking of you>"* Thoreau

*"Invest a few moments in thinking. It will pay good interest."
Robert Holden. P.h.D. Physiologist.*

*"It is the mark of educated mind to be able
to entertain a thought without accepting it."* Aristotle.

***I mean well there for I do good, that makes me a good person,
if you appose me you do not mean well and therefore you
can't be a good person. <u>This is very bad thinking.</u>***

***

THINKING
POSITIVELY IS A MUST

Happy thoughts make life so much better.

You must think about happy events in the past.

*Looking back gives us a sense of where we have been
and how we got where were are.*
Matt Johnson Ph.d

Realistic hope is good.

Hoping realistically can often make one motivated
to materialize the hope.

Hope can pushes us to take action if we let it.

Positive people have more energy and more
self-confidence and are more hopeful.

Positive people are more resilient , which
helps them bounce back and persevere
despite setbacks.

***

EVIL

Birds of a feather flock together.
Evil is driven by lack of emotions, shame and empathy,
probably lack of love as a child.
Excessive preoccupation with one self
often leads to evil acts.
Don't let a evil person live in your mind.
Evil has to be eliminated or dealt with
at its conception and must not be permitted to grow.

Drugs can do damage to the brain and make a person evil;
they damage the part of the brain that we use for empathy.
Profound immorality is considered Evil.

*"All that is necessary for the triumph of evil,
is that good men do nothing." Edmond Burke. (1729 - 1797)*

"Evil usually done in the name of goodness."
*"Those who don't fight **the greatest evils**
will fight lesser evils or make believe evils."*
*"History teaches us only the naive
believe people are basically good." Dennis Prager.*

People are evil, when they, lie, cheat, hurt others,
both physically and mentally and don't care about you.
People are evil when they use you
as a objects to be manipulated, for their gain.
If you have a evil person
in your life, <u>have nothing to do with them.</u>
★★★★

RATIONALIZING

Rationalizing is
using one's emotions
instead of intellect;
it gives a person
explanations and justifications
and allows one not to prove.

Rationalization lets you escape morality,
responsibility and indulge in one's imperfections.

Rationalization stops your using your thinking ability.

<u>Always use your brain and power of reason.</u>

*"Looking ahead is more important
than looking behind you."*
Victor Davis Hanson.

*"Rationalization is a process not perceiving reality
but of attempting to make reality fit one's emotions."*
Ayn Rand.

*"Rationalization may be defined as
self-deception by reasoning."*
Karen Horney.

***

SUFFERING

"Suffering as such is not a value;
only man's fight against suffering is."
Ayn Rand.

Suffering is a choice.
Learn not to suffer.
If you accept suffering as a natural part of your existence,
it will make you more tolerant to adversities in your life.

Look for the good in your suffering
and capitalize on it; often it is hard to find.
Making changes helps suffering.
One has to be patient when suffering;
time is often the best healer.
Mindful meditation helps suffering.
When choosing to help a person suffering
do it for their moral goodness their
virtue and feel good that you helped someone in need.

Helping those fighting to recover
who are suffering unjustly, in a helpless situation,
will bring you great pleasure now and in the future.

Tell a person suffering you are there for them
they can depend on you and they can call you any time.

Make the best of anything.
***

ATTITUDE

"Weakness of attitude becomes
weakness of character."
Albert Einstein.

Your attitude is very important to life,
because it governs your emotions, beliefs and behaviors
toward yourself and other and your life.

Life is full of disappointments we have to live with them.
Disappointments "This to shall pass" King Solomon

This book should improve your attitude.

"Weakness of attitude becomes weakness of character."
Albert Einstein.

"The winner's edge is not in a gifted birth,
a high IQ or in talent.
The winners edge is all in the attitude not aptitude.
Attitude is the criterion for success. "
Denis Waitley.

Always work on improving your attitude,
a must in today's society.

In the end it the one with a great
attitude who succeeds.
***

FEAR / ANXIETY
"There is light at the end of the tunnel."

Fear is very powerful.

Fear often starts at child hood we fear our parents and teachers.

If anxious; calm yourself by breathing deeply.

Look for the good, look for options.

Laughing out loud helps anxiety.

Fear based behavior spins out of control
and becomes addictive.

Fear and Anxiety are a basic emotions.
<u>You must conquer irrational fear, replace it with
Courage and Reason. Never fear making an error.</u>

"The only thing we have to fear is fear itself." F. Roosevelt.

Fear of what is coming next tends to bring irrational
thoughts. Fear due to danger is an automatic reflex.

*"Fear is a vital response to physical and emotional danger-
if we didn't feel it, we couldn't protect ourselves from
legitimate threats. But often we fear situations that are far
from life-or-death, and thus hang back for no good reason."*
Psychology Today

**Anxiety can make one improve performance,
because we don't want to remain anxious.**

Being fearful can stop you from moving ahead.

Don't be overwhelmed by the fear of lack of love,
negativity, being neglected and not getting what you want.

Reject from your thoughts and conquer, fear and rejection.
Conquer guilt, self-pity, envy, anger, hate,
sadness, regret and disappointment.

Don't be fearful of making wrong choices.

**Often information, sometimes true but often inaccurate,
creates fears which can be accepted or rejected.**

Don't be afraid of conflict because you are probably right.

Don't be fearful of not being good enough.

<u>When fearful, anxious reach out to another for support.
Asking for help is a strength not a weakness.</u>

"Have a healthy fear of parents, teachers, authorities."
"Rational fear is O.K. Irrational Fear is bad." Denis Prager.

Don't be fearful that you're selfish if you want happiness for yourself.

Fear of the unknown and the future impedes some
not to make decisions. Don't be one of these people.

**Sometime we have to overcome fear
when we are in a risky situation.**

Remember fear keeps us safe when we cross the street.

Do not fear being assaulted or robbed.

Fear can keep you vigilant, moral and social.

Fear can simulate what is wrong and how to deal with it.

Fear can damage you and those close to you.

A little Anxiety can make you act to solve the problem
and improve performance. Sometimes taking
risks and dealing with adversity can teach us our potential.

Without fear we can be uncritical and a risk taker.

We came into this world without fear,
we learned to walk without fear of falling down,
we did not believe we could not walk.

If you have panic attacks, phobias get professional help.

<u>The best antidote to fear is Reason.</u>
<u>Humor is the antidote to fear and bad anxiety.</u>

Don't have a resentment that others have more than you.
***

WORRY

is not productive.
Worry can effect your health.
People worry too much
because they think something bad will happen.
Don't worry be concerned look for solutions.

*"When I look back on all the worries I had in my life
most never happened."* Winston Churchill.

For some worry makes them take action
and eliminate the worry.
For others it effects their health and well being.

Life is uncertain; we have to live with that.
People who don't worry have the ability
to stay in the present.

One worry can start another worry.
Ask yourself what is the worst that could happen?

Exercise helps when you are worried.
Write the problem down, tear it up, get rid of it.
Talk it over with your best friend.

*"Worry does not empty tomorrow of its sorrow,
it empties today of its strength."* Leo Buscaglia.

Worry about important things, then take action.
***

STRESS
Remember <u>stress is bad.</u>

Stress is a feeling of emotional or
physical tension.
Stress can come from any event or thought
that make you feel frustrated ,angry, or nervous.

Stress is your body's reaction to a challenge or demand.

Stress can make you physically sick
causing, depression, bad moods, heart trouble,
eating disorders and memory loss, etc.

In small doses stress can help you perform
under pressure and motivate you to do your best.

To eliminate stress:
Get plenty of sleep 8 hours minimum.
go to bed at the same time each night.

Take a nap in the afternoon if possible.

Have a close relationship with someone.

<u>When you don't have credit card debt, car payments
or a mortgage payment you don't have money stress.</u>

<u>Always have money for emergencies.</u>

Breathe deeply often.

Have a healthy Diet (Mediterranean)
Vegetables and Fruit.

~EXERCISE.~is a must.
Meditate - Do Deep breathing..
in order to not be stressed out.

Read a book. - Go for a walk. - Have Hobbies.
helps eliminate stress.

Routine eliminates stress and anxiety.

Green live plants help reduce stress
and induce good moods.

Have plants outside your windows
and inside your home and office.

Reach out for support,
talk to a friend, spend time with them.

Don't guess what is on some one mind
because it can be stressful..

What's stressful for you may be quite different
from what's stressful to someone els.

When you are out of control don't latch on
to predicting the worst possible outcome, be positive.

Laugh in private as a means of emotional relief.

Focus on the present, enjoy the moment.

Learn what causes stress in your life and eliminate it.

Make changes.

Write the problem down that is causing your stress,
mail it or destroy it; this act helps you deal with stress.

*"The greatest weapon against stress is our ability
to choose one thought over another."William James.*

*"Adopting the right attitude can convert a negative stress
into a positive one." Hans Selye.*

"Worry is not only futile, it poisons the present."
Karl Andrew Pillemer.

Stress is thinking about the bad past events, or bad
future events.
Thinking about **happy events** in the past is better.

I repeat - Daily Excise is the answer to stress anxiety
and many other complaints.

Some times we just have to say "So What !"

***

CONFIDENCE

You can always improve you confidence by
turning thoughts into ability, good judgement,
then taking action and risks.

Mastering, experiencing and learning brings confidence.
Often mentors give us confidence.
This book *"Life is Simple book"* is a confidence builder.

You must be confident to stand up
to those who would mentally and physically abuse you.
People who are not confident rely on approval from others.

"No one can make you feel inferior without your consent."
Eleanor Roosevelt.

"When you have confidence, you can have a lot of fun.
And when you have fun, you can do amazing things."
Joe Namath.

Work on your attitude every day
will dictate your behavior; and bring great results.
<u>Say every morning; "I am going to enjoy today."</u>

Believe in yourself.
It is never too late to believe in yourself.
Take control of your life.
Stand up straight.
****

FAILURE

Be aware how your mind reacts to failure.
Our brain can be convinced, by even one failure,
that we can't succeed and it makes us a negative person.

Just hearing from someone we believe in, that we can't
do something, can be enough to convince us we will fail.

When our mind is made up to fail, it is hard to make
the necessary changes to succeed and to try again.
You cannot allow yourself
to become convinced you can't succeed.

You have to gain control and break negative cycles.
You must tell yourself **<u>twenty five times</u> over and over,**
YOU CAN,
when you know you have the ability.

If your mind convinces you that you are incapable,
you could get the feeling of helplessness
and you won't reach your potential.
Once you become convinced of something
it is hard to change your mind.

Many people succeed when they fail often.
Try using several answers one will work, diversify.
Use your intuition, if you programed your brain well.
Always use the word **CAN**, never can't!
***

APPRECIATION

**Don't take anything, or any person for granted;
especially good deeds.**

Tell loved one's and friends you appreciate them.
Carry out acts of kindness.

Appreciate and be grateful for the good things
and people in your life.
Appreciate what you have, not what you want.

Take very good care of people and things in your life
that you appreciate, especially you.
Sharing requires appreciation.

Appreciate your faculties, touch, smell, sight,
your use of your hands, your brain, your imagination,
all of which can't be duplicated by robots.

*"Appreciation is a wonderful thing.
It makes what is excellent in others belong to us as well."*
Voltaire.

Don't forget to say *"Thank you."* with a smile.
Take the time to compliment.
Take the time to write a complimentary letter.
You must appreciate your friends
and loved one's and tell them.
***

VALUE

The best things in life are free value them.

*"The most important thing you will ever have
is good values." Dennis Prager*

Value defines us and is very important in life.

Value authenticity and the truth.

*"Your values are the things that you believe
are important; in the way you live and work,
they should determine your priorities."*
Sarah Pavey.

Our values control our subconscious emotions.

Understanding your values will tell you
if your life is working the way you want.

"Price is what you pay: value is what you get."
Patrick Morris. (Motley Fool)

What constitutes value is interest.

You have to be ethical to value.

Always get value.
Value human talent, abilities and inventions.

Value yourself and deserve to live.

Our conscious is a measuring stick like our values.

Your own needs and values matter,
despite what others expect.

To value oneself is the basis in being
able to value others.

You must learn or know how to value people
and things before you put them in your life.

If you know how something is made
you can value it better.

*"Values are the motivating power of man's
actions and a necessity of his survival, psychologically
as well as physically." Ayn Rand.*

VALUE MORAL AND ETHICAL PEOPLE

Good Brains can make you a Scientist a Doctor,
and they are abundant
Common sense and values are hard to find. ,

**Remember feelings are not Values
you can decide what values to hold.**

***

RELATIONSHIPS

You must have a healthy relationship
with yourself before you can have a healthy
with relationship with others.

"What I love about you is everything you have that I don't."
Unknown Author.

Don't look for someone like yourself,
look for what is missing, what you do not have,
to compliment your relationship.

MEN: Want the feminine brought to a relationship.
WOMEN: Want the masculinity brought to a relationship.

Great relationships get better as years roll on.
Never take anyone for granted.

"A friend to all is a friend to none". Aristotle.

*"Good relationships keep us happier
and healthier Period." Harvards 75 year study.*

You must have a best friend in your life.
You must be able to count on your friends
and love one's, when you need them.

If a aggressive partner sets the rules, your
relationship will be in trouble.

**You must care about your relationship
and never be jealous.**

Unhappy people have trouble with relationships.
Cultivate quality, healthy, close relationships.

<u>Long distance relationships seldom work</u>

Obsessive passion is not good;
you need harmonious passion in a relationship.
Each person must be happy
giving their fair share to the relationship.

Supportive, family, friends, social relationships
are all good for us.

If you don't connect with your genuine <u>good </u>family
do it, you will be healthier and happier
if they are supportive people.

SHARING brings extra joy to activities
also when you share possessions.

Laughter in a relationships is a <u>must.</u>

Loneliness kills.
Social connections are really good for us.

Say **"NO"** to avoid being controlled.
Always use the **power of " NO"** in your life.
Your relationship has to be built on trust.

**Get involved with people that leave you
feeling better than before you encountered them.**

Writing your deepest thoughts about your relationship
makes the relationship last longer.

The extent to which you know the minute details
of your partner's life is a good predictor
of how long your relationship will last.

If knowing your partners life creates jealousy get help.

Commitment is important for relationship, longevity
because it will lead to doing or saying the right things.

Spend more time looking for the good
in people than the bad.

Don't let your relationship become boring.

Breaking up the routine is essential.

Engaging in novel and exciting activities,
going on adventures helps relationships.

Enjoy a date with your wife or husband often.

Talking to a good friend about your troubles, your
fears, is good for you; it is not good keeping it in.

Never help others at your expense.

Write your troubles down on paper to get it out of you.

*"I think without the feeling of affection and connection
with other fellow human beings, life becomes very hard."*
Dali Lama.

Are you satisfied in your relationship?
You must be able to coexist with your friends and
partners' imperfections.

Ask how are you emotionally in your relationships?
Ask your partner often what they need from you.
Good relationships keep us happier and healthier.
Bad conflicts in marriages is worse than divorce.

Do not forget to sincerely compliment
and show your love by your actions.

*"There isn't time, so brief is life,
for bickering apologies heartburning, call in to
account there is only time for loving. "*   *Mark Twain.*

The most important word is LOVE.
The quality of your close relationship is all that matters.

*Health is the greatest gift, contentment the
greatest wealth, faithfulness the best relationship. Buddha.*
Be a cheerleader in your relationships.
Fulfill your obligation to your relationships.
***

CARING - EMPATHY
COMPASSION

**How much emphasis you put into caring,
empathy, gratitude, serving, sharing and compassion
complimenting, should depend on your philosophy.**

Without caring, empathy and compassion
in your philosophy you certainly
will be less happy than you could be.

Happy people care about their work,
their loved one's, friends and their possessions
and do not hurt others feelings.

Make certain people believe you care.

Keep a pack of 'Thank You Notes' handy.

You must care for and appreciate
important things in your life.

Have plenty of caring and love in your life.

A non-caring relationship will not work.

Caring and compassion for oneself, about what you do,
is an important ingredient in your drive to success.

Helping others is very satisfying.

**Compassion should be used
for innocent victims, never for those
who do acts of evil, such as torturers.**

Without compassion, you will be
looked on negatively and be far less
happy than most people are.

Moral, dignified people are,
compassionate and caring.

When you greet someone treat everyone
the same way, caring and cordially,
whether they are rich or poor or famous.

Our reflexes make us judge people.
Our biases in our subconscious can mislead us.

When we meet someone we automatically read their
body language and decide if they are friend or foe.
We mirror a persons expression; if they are sad
we take on a sad expression and become sad,
and show compassion.

If they are happy
we take on a happy expression and feel good,
and show happiness to be with them.

Feeling grateful will bring you joy.

Treat yourself well, like you want to be treated.

Enhance your compassion toward others.

"Empathy uses the same parts
of the brain as when we are in pain."
David England. P.B.S.

"Caring for but never trying to own
may be a further way to define friendship."
William Gasser.

Some only realize what others are going through,
when they experience the same event.

Imagine others pain and you will be more
sympathetic to their pain.

Lack of compassion, is very detrimental
to happiness, romance and friendships.

"It's not what you said to me,
it's how you made me feel." *Frank Luntz.*

"No act of kindness, no matter how small, is ever wasted."
Aesop
"Wisdom, Compassion, and Courage
are the three universally recognized moral qualities of me."Confucius.

Compliment truthfully people you meet, also friends and lovers.
When you complement others it makes you also feel good.
***

MENTORS

**It is always good to have someone in
your life to encourage you.**

*"A mentor is is someone who sees more talent and
ability within you, than you see in yourself,
and helps bring it out of you."*
Bob Proctor.

Mentors often recognize your potential
when you fail to see it.

It seems happy and successful people
all had mentors in their life.

If you don't have a Mentor
maybe it is time to reach out to find someone.

*"The key is to keep company only
with people who uplift you, whose presence
calls forth your best."*
Epictetus.

*"A lot of people have gone further than they thought
they could because someone else thought they could."*

***

PREDICTORS OF SUCCESS

*"Passion - Determination - Talent -
Self-discipline - Faith."*
AARP Magazine.

Really wan't to do it.
Courage to make it a happen.
Caring and happy about what you do.
> **Success must be your own idea and your definition.** <

To be successful you need these
characteristics:
APTITUDE - MOTIVATION - OPTIMISM - PERSISTANT

YOU MUST BE:
COMPETITIVE - POISED - CONFIDENT - SKILLED
SELF- CONTROLLED - ALERT - ENTHUSIASTIC
DISCIPLINED - FOCUSED - PASSIONATE -
DO GOOD

YOU MUST HAVE:
Endurance - resilience - push - purpose -
trust courage - goals.
AND HAVE FUN
A LOVE FOR WHAT YOU DO.
BE HAPPY.

PROMOTION GOES TO THOSE WHO ARE THE BEST.

**Don't lose faith.
Don't try to be what your not.**

IF YOU DON'T KNOW YOUR PRIORITIES
YOU DON'T HAVE PRIORITIES.

The only thing that keeps successful people going is
their love for what they are doing
and the people they love.

Find out what you love to do and who you love.

Work fills a large part of our lives,
and the only way to be truly satisfied
is to do what you believe is great work.

The only way to do great work is to
<u>love what you do.</u>
If you have not found it, keep looking.
As with all matters of the heart,
you'll know when you find it!

You need a little dose of pessimism and
a big dose of optimism and
time and patience to succeed.

*"Many of life's failures are people who did not realize
how close they were to success when they gave up."*
Thomas Edison.

GET IN THE GAME BECAUSE YOU ARE NEEDED.

Successful people learn and use, push,
effort perseverance, persistence,
they talk to themselves.

PRACTICE MAKES PERFECT

<u>You are successful when it is your own ideas.</u>

When repeating a task do it better the next time.
the improvement makes it more interesting
and more satisfying.

*"Success is the ability to go from one failure
to another with no loss of enthusiasm."*
Winston Churchill.

Obstacles to success are in the
unconscious part of our Brains.

Don't let emotions take over us reason.

*"The measure of success is not whether you have
a tough problem to deal with but whether it's the
same problem you had last year."* *John Foster Dulles.*

"Be so good they can't ignore you." *Steve Martin.*

Be kind and courteous; don't interrupt people
and listen to others to learn.

You have to put in the work to be the best.

Except blame and give credit.
The road to success is paved with pitfalls this should
make you have the courage to overcome.
Ten years of constant practice and consistent learning
will put you on the path to becoming world class.

**The following ingredients
are necessary to be <u>the very best.</u>**
Purpose, Deep Passion, Learning, Planing, Focus.
More practice, More effort. More Sacrifice, More action.
Demonstrating courage.Wanting more. Generating energy.
Working harder, increasing productivity.Meaningful work.
Reward and curiosity.Seeking clarity of your purpose.

Always choose well.
Loosing matters, it makes you overcome, and succeed.
Have good people skills. Champion others.
Develop a good influence with people;
will get you on your way to world class.

~

Most people do not want to be world class,
which often means putting off a balanced
life and giving up many things.
<u>You must ask </u>what are the consequences
of your actions does it justify your actions?
Remember there is always someone better than you.
Rewards don't go to those who do their best
but to those who succeed.
***

MOTIVATION
Action~Persistance~Intensity

Saying and thinking I will spend only
five minutes doing something I am not
motivated to do, will get you started.
After five minutes
you will find it easier to continue.

Old habits are your obstacles.
Reward yourself when you have achieved
what you set out to do.
Take small steps then big steps will follow.

"What makes life dreary is the want of a motive."
George Eliot.

"If you are coasting your going down hill."
Donald Rumfield.

TO BE MOTIVATED IS TO BE IN PURSUIT OF A REALISTIC GOAL.

Be specific about what you want to achieve.
Setting the bar high and reasonable is important.
Unconsciously, difficult goals, often make you
increase your effort, focus more, and
use reason to accomplish your goals.

Get stuff done, have fun and accomplish great things.

Do the best your capable of doing.
Face up to your obstacles.
Make yourself indispensable.
Motivation is often fleeting comes and goes
and can be unreliable.

We get motivated when we decide to direct our own lives.
We have to have the desire to get better and better.

Doing something that matters is a great motivator.
We are motivated into action when we believe.

Often doing something larger than ourselves,
gives us a motivation to do it.
Make the chore seem like fun.
Northing ventured nothing gained.

"If you can dream it, you can do it."Walt Disney.

"The secret of getting ahead is to get started."   *Mark Twain.*

"Looking ahead is more important than looking behind you"
                              Victor Davis Hansan.

Sex can be a motivator and often ends badly.

As we get older we tend to procrastinate.
Be in charge and recharge your motivation
"Better late than never."
***

CHOICES / DECISIONS

CHOICES & DECISIONS ARE THE MOST
IMPORTANT THING WE DO IN LIFE.

Make rational choices and decisions.

Takes courage to make good choices.

You will get pleasure choosing well.

**To know if it is the right thing to do;
ask yourself what happens if every one did it?**

**Remember everything we choose has
consequences good or bad.**

Value truth over emotions and feelings.

**Avoid excess or extremes especially
in ones behavior.**

*"Is there any one of us who has never resorted to excuses
about his circumstances when he has done wrong
or made a bad decision." Anthony Daniels.*

Don't make choices or decisions
when you are tired or feel emotional.

**In this world, even in what appears
to be the most perfect situation, imperfections
might exist, in spite of such, you must make the best
possible choice for yourself.**

Life is full of trade off's.

Use the power of reason, together with
your philosophy, your wisdom and your ethics
to make the best choices or decisions.

**You should consider the consequences of your
choice in ten minutes, ten months, and ten years.**

Remember when you choose you often give up something,
something you enjoy or value.

You may have to make changes and different choices based
on new truths and facts; as you learn them.

The unintentional consequences of our choices
often tip the scale away from the intended good.

The uncertainty of change and chance
often leads to a good outcome.

Do not be overwhelmed by information.

To much information will make you choose from
the last thing you learnt.

IDENTIFY WHY YOU MAKE BAD CHOICES.

"Where there is a will there is a way." Unknown.

People faced with too many choices
are apt to make no decisions at all.

Doing nothing is less risky, doing something is better.

Good balance between emotion and reason seems
to give the best result, when making choices.

If you can't pin point what works for you,
write three possible solutions and try them all.

Think hard before you decide: use <u>reason.</u>

<u>Remember everything in life is a choice.</u>

<u>**Ask how much you pay and how much it will cost you?**</u>

**It might sound great, is it practicable,
is it reasonable, does it make it better or worse?**

Don't blame others when you make bad
choices for yourself.

Look at the problem from a distance
it won't be so overwhelming.

Does it make sense?

**You don't have to do it to know what it is like;
you can use your imagination to
visualize bad and good things.**

When you come to a fork in the road and don't know
where you are going it doesn't matter which fork you take.

Don't follow like the heard mentality do,
don't be like a Sheep and follow the crowd.
Make up your own mind
based on truth and facts.

*"We don't get to choose what is true.
We only get to choose what we do about it. Kami Garcia.*

Every thing in life is a choice especially your happiness.
You choose to be happy or unhappy.

*"When it comes to making life changing decisions,
neither snap judgement or sleeping on it
trumps good old fashioned conscious thought."*
Live Science.

Sometimes it is wise to give it another chance.

Judge it, is it good or evil?

"If in doubt leave it out."
***

LUCK

~

Do what the lucky people do.
Here are the nineteen things lucky people have in common.

They love living.
They strive to improve.
They have a sense of humor.
They love life and laugh a lot
They take risks and are flexible.
They assume fate is on their side.
They keep envy and jealousy in check.
They are very friendly and trust people.
They are happy and enjoy life and people.
They never try using supernatural powers.
They wan't to hear what people have to say.
They keep their mind open to opportunities.
They have no fear of theft or negative things.
They have high energy to get what they want.
They get to know as many people as they can.
They are focused they use their brain and reason.
They have their negative emotions under control.
They are well balanced, optimistic and have courage.
They have a mentor or someone who pushes them up.

~

**The more often you read and digest this book
the luckier you will become.**

LUCKY PEOPLE
ADD SOMETHING NEW TO THEIR LIVES.
Lucky people treat everyone well.
Lucky people treat everyone the same way.
Lucky people cut down looking at TV
the Computer and their Phone.

Lucky people cut down sitting,
which can effect their health.
Lucky people get up off
the couch during commercials.

Lucky people look for a critic
to get alternative views.

Lucky people understand
Randomness of nature.

Lucky people never
let fear stop them from making decisions.

Remember you can't do more than your best.

*"The amount of good luck coming
your way depends on your willingness to act."*
                                        Barbara Sher.

***

YOUR HEALTH
Please pay attention to your health.

HEALTH IS EXTREMELY IMPORTANT FOR YOUR WELL BEING AND HAPPINESS.

Without good health you can't be happy.
When we are young we take our good health for granted.

When visiting your Doctor smile; you will be treated well.

<u>Moderate</u> **Exercise Meditation (Page 71) Deep Breathing,**
is one of the keys to good health,
Do Exercise, Meditate, Do deep breathing often.

Eat healthy too improve your brain and body,
Mediterranean Diet is excellent for your Body and Brain
Beans, Nuts, & Green Vegetables Vitamins

"You can't have a healthy mind without a healthy Gut."
T Dinan

Many brain functions depend on what you eat.

Learn what you can eat and what you can't eat.

Do <u>deep breathing daily, in through your nose,
out through your mouth,</u>
this is very good for body and mind.

Mindful Meditation keeps your mind healthy.
As do dancing, writing and solving puzzles.

A lot of our good health depends on our belief
You must have a happy healthy attitude.

<u>Say to yourself often;</u>
"I will be healthy in body and mind."

You brain is connected to your immune system.
Poor thinking impedes the immune system.

**YOUR HAPPINESS IS THE BEST MEDICINE
LAUGHING EVERY DAY PUTS
YOU IN A GOOD MOOD..**

Conflict is bad for health.

Educate yourself about your medical condition.

Remember anxiety is temporary, stay calm and relaxed.
Be courageous.

Likable people tend to live longer and have healthier lives.
Vitamin C is needed to convert Dopamine to Serotonin.

*"If you believe your brain can cure your ailments, it will.
This is called a placebo effect.
<u>BrainFacts.org</u>>mood>articles."*
***

THE DECLARATION OF ***INDEPENDENCE ***

We are all created equal........
"....Life Liberty and the
PURSUIT OF HAPPINESS."

"God grant me the Serenity to accept the things
I cannot change......
the courage to change the things I can.....
the wisdom to know the difference."

*"Most folks are as happy as they
make up their minds to be."*

*"With the fearful strain that is on me night and
day if I did not **laugh** I should die." Abraham Lincoln.*

"You create your own universe as you go along."
Winston Churchill.

It is easy to judge the mistakes of others
but difficult to recognize our own mistakes.

*"The two most important days in life are the day you are
born and the day you discover the reason why." Mark Twain.*

*Jefferson said: "When the people fears the Government that is Tyranny.
When the Government fear the people that is Liberty."*